To my father and to Claire,
My September companions.
A. V.

To Julie and P.P., especially...
And to Grégoire and Fanette.
B. B.

«I do not think of myself as an adult. I think of myself as someone who, every morning, gets up like a fool who has to get through the day.»

A fool? Him? Le Corbusier, the greatest architect of the twentieth century!

Perhaps that is why he is such an assiduous worker, such a furious writer, a man who grasps every opportunity to put his ideas into practice. He built his first house when he was seventeen, and from then until his death, he never stopped building. He ran into storms of criticism and torrents of abuse, but he kept on going because he had a vision. The vision of a rapidly emerging new society: the machine age, the machinist civilisation.

There were great changes in the world during the nineteenth century. The possibilities offered by technical innovation, steel, concrete, and scientific progress opened up new possibilities for architects and engineers engaged in building. Le Corbusier looked around him and saw cars, gigantic liners that crossed the oceans, and even aircraft that flew in the sky. None of this would have been possible without scientific progress. But if such progress could completely revolutionise transport (the carts and carriages still in use just twenty years previously had nothing in common with the motor cars beginning to fill city streets at the beginning of the century), why couldn't it be applied to houses, to buildings, and, more generally, to cities?

One of Le Corbusier's most famous pronouncements, the one that gave rise to the most attacks and misunderstandings was: «The house is a machine for living in». What did he mean? Were houses to be invaded by machines and become like miniature factories? Were all houses to look like factory housing and be plain, dull and dismal? Not at all. Le Corbusier had an extremely human vision of his profession as an architect. For him architecture must be at the service of humans and families, it must facilitate daily life and the relationships between the people living in the houses; it must provide a comfortable, relaxing home for everyone. And each element must be designed as a well-oiled mechanism: the way the sun comes through the windows, the sound-proofing, the location of the garage, each element must follow precise rules. And because, in the modern world, a house rarely stands alone, he was interested in towns and how they were organised. He worked as a town planner.

He devised plans for reorganising Paris, then Algiers, then São Paolo, and finally built them in India, in Chandigarh, the capital city of the Punjab. There, at the foot of the Himalayas, he built a modern city that met all the criteria he had set out.

Le Corbusier's influence was immense and is still a determining influence on the architectural profession today.

Antoine Vigne

Le Corbusier

Devised by Antoine Vigne

Illustrated by Betty Bone

Sponsored by Fondation Le Corbusier

PAPADAKIS

One of my (extraordinary) teachers
steered me gently away from a mediocre fate.
He wanted to make an architect of me.

I hated architecture and architects.

My father [...] was passionate about the
mountains and the river around us. [...]
We constantly climbed peaks. [...] My
adolescence was characterised by an insatiable
curiosity. I knew what flowers were like, both
inside and out, the shape and colour of birds. I
understood how trees grew and how it was that
they could withstand storms; and the cycle of
water, rain, evaporation, clouds, and storms.

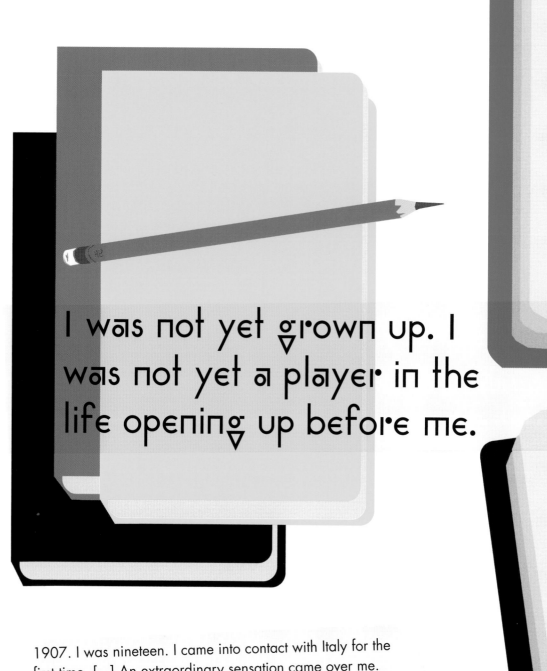

I was not yet grown up. I was not yet a player in the life opening up before me.

Architecture, pure creation of the mind... The Parthenon – a machine to rouse the emotions.

1907. I was nineteen. I came into contact with Italy for the first time. [...] An extraordinary sensation came over me. I experienced the fulfilment of true human aspirations: silence, solitude; but also, relationships (daily contact) with other mortals: and I even experienced the demonstration of what is imperceptible.

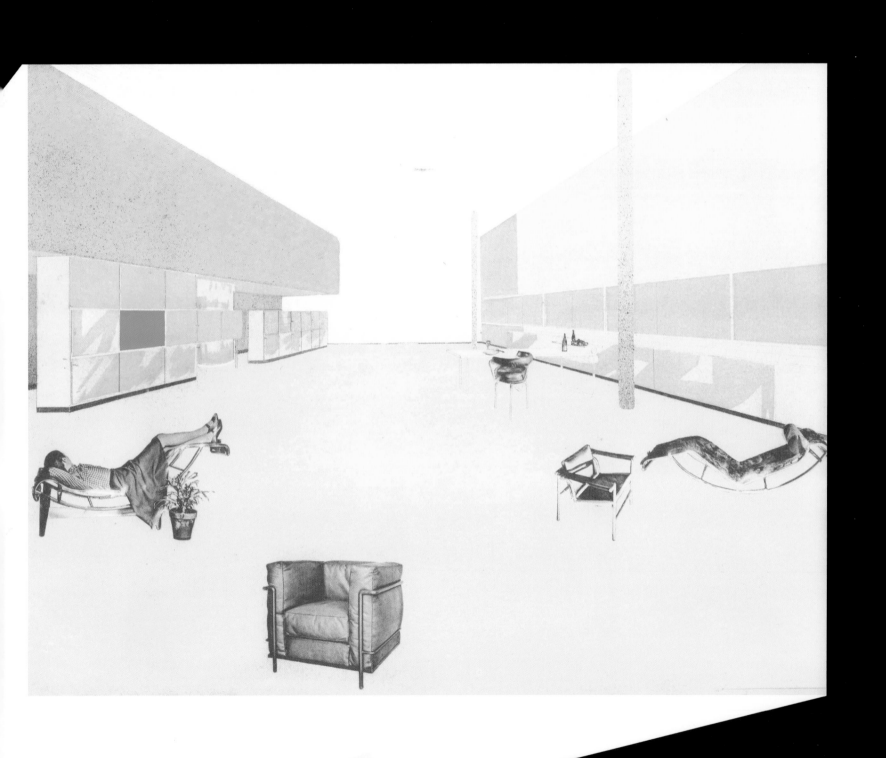

Art exists. Decorative art does not.

Where order reigns, well-being follows.

Houses should no longer be built by the metre but by the kilometre.

Sun, space, trees: that is what all cities need.

The world is full of blemishes called big cities.

Being born, eating, dressing, enjoying the life-giving force of love and friendship. Somewhere to live is the most important. Working or getting around are incidental. The house is the key.

The Radiant City

Once we have understood, architecture will follow.

Through our brothers, separated from us by the silence of an ocean, I have understood the scrupules, the doubts, the hesitation and the reasons behind their present work and I have put my trust in the future. Once we have understood, architecture will follow.

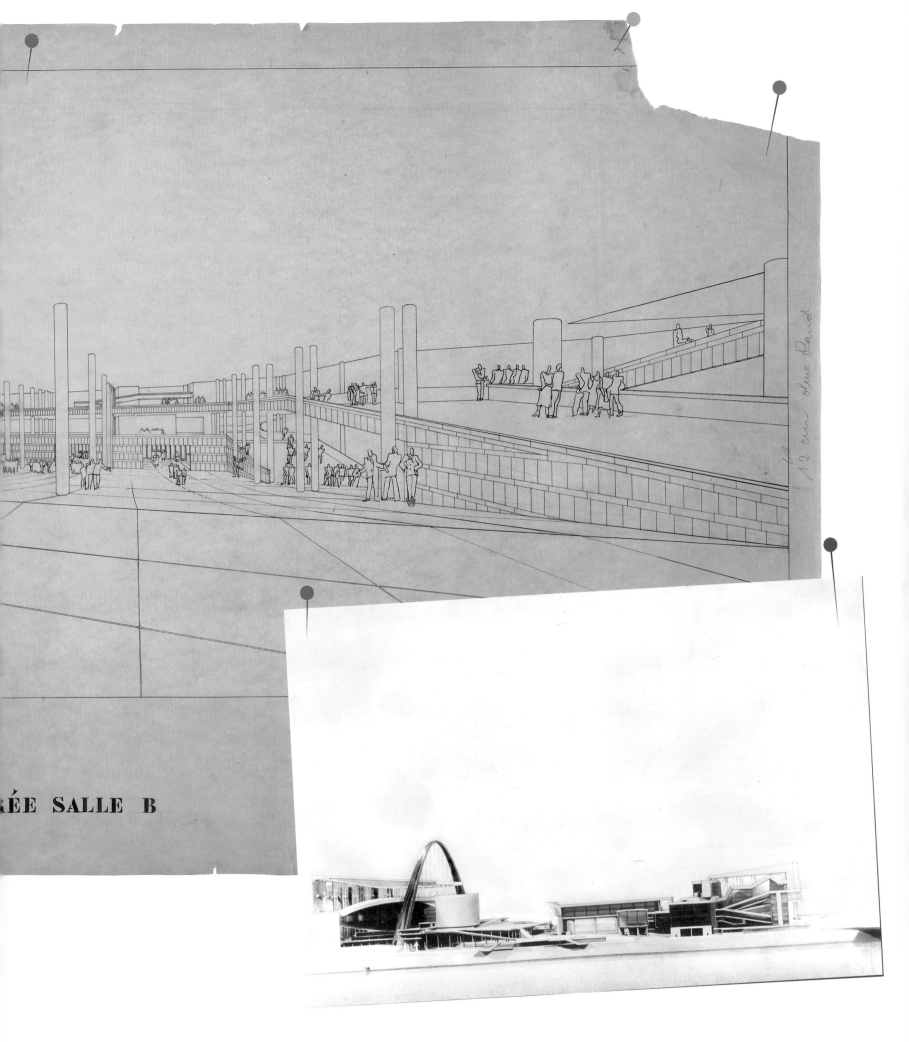

RÉE SALLE B

I shall always be convinced that humans are active beings in a world in action; they are not a passive element. The fakir told me himself.

Le Corbusier is one of the greatest, if not the greatest architect of the twentieth century. He greatly influenced what is called Modernism in architecture, not only through his buildings but also through his prolific writings.

6-7 : Childhood. Le Corbusier, real name Charles-Édouard Jeanneret, was born on 6 October 1887, in La Chaux-de-Fonds, Switzerland. His father was an enameller of watch faces. When Le Corbusier was thirteen and a half he became an apprentice engraver of watch cases. His teacher, called L'Eplattenier, was a critical influence on his life and career. It was he who steered him towards architecture, despite the initial reluctance of his pupil.

8-9, 10-11 : Formative years / sketch books and first houses. In 1905, Charles-Édouard Jeanneret built his first house, the Villa Fallet, at La Chaux-de-Fonds in Switzerland. He was seventeen and a half. He used the fees he was paid to travel to Italy where he visited Pisa, Florence, Siena, Ravenna, Padua, Ferrara and Verona. Then he went on to Budapest and Vienna, where he spent the winter. Finally, he went to Paris, where he arrived in March 1908, where he worked in the office of the famous architect Auguste Perret. He continued on his travels, first to Germany and then he decided to head for the Orient. During the next seven months he passed though Serbia, Romania, Bulgaria, and as far as Istanbul and Athens. This journey – but especially the sight of the Parthenon in Athens – had a profound influence on his work. During the First World War, Jeanneret began to think about the production of mass housing in order to solve the problems associated with reconstruction. This resulted in the Dom-Ino houses. Then he built a house that revealed the orginality of his architecture, the Villa Schwob. Unlike traditional houses in which the interior walls support the structure, this villa is built on four pillars and the interior walls serve only to separate the spaces inside.

12-13 : "L'Esprit nouveau". Appearance on the international scene. On 15th October 1920, Le Corbusier published the first number of "L'Esprit nouveau" (The New Spirit), an international magazine on contemporary art, with his friend, the painter Amédée Ozenfant. The magazine brought him international fame. It was in this magazine that he used the name Le Corbusier for the first time.

14-15 : Towards a new architecture. In 1923, Le Corbusier collected together various articles that had appeared in "L'Esprit nouveau" and published them in a book with the title *Towards a New Architecture*. This book still constitutes today one of the seminal texts of modern architecture. At the same time, he opened his own practice in Paris with his cousin Pierre Jeanneret.

16-17 : Art. Le Corbusier began to paint around 1918. Painting always played an important part in his life. There were numerous painters in his circle, including Amédée Ozenfant and Fernand Léger.

18-19 : The modern dwelling: the machine for living in. In 1925, Le Corbusier designed the "Esprit nouveau" pavilion, as part of the 1925 Decorative Arts exhibition in Paris. This pavilion exhibited the characteristics of what he called a machine for living in just as an aeroplane was a machine for flying in. He applied very strict rules to the layout so that it would fulfil the needs of the inhabitants in their daily life. He then built several houses based on the same criteria. The most famous one is the Villa Savoy at Poissy, near Paris.

20-21 : The decorative arts. Le Corbusier's ideas on architecture quite naturally led him to become interested in the elements that constitute the interior of a house, especially those elements that belong to the field of the decorative arts. With his friends Charlotte Perriand and Amédée Ozenfant, he designed furniture that he exhibited at the Decorative Arts exhibition in Paris in 1929. One of his most important books is: "The Decorative Art of Today".

22-23 : The city with three million inhabitants and the Voisin plan for Paris. But Le Corbusier was not only an architect. His vision extended to organising the city: to town planning. He worked on his plan for a city of three million inhabitants from the beginning of the 1920s. In this plan, he proposed a rational organisation of the city, separating residential areas from industrial areas, and he applied a great deal of energy to separating traffic flows from routes reserved for pedestrians.

24-25 : Tomorrow's city / the Radiant City. Le Corbusier found himself the object of the derision of many critics who denounced his authoritative vision and saw in his plans the destruction of the traditional city. But he stuck to his position and maintained that tomorrow's city, the city for the modern world would justify the name "Radiant City." He produced numerous plans for Algiers in Algeria and São Paulo in Brazil.

26-27 : Travel, lectures in the United States and Russia, the Centrosoyuz, the Salvation Army Refuge in Paris, joint work and influence. Soon Le Corbusier had invitations to lecture all over the world. He built many buildings such as the Centrosoyuz in Moscow, the Swiss Pavilion in the Cité Universitaire in Paris and the Salvation Army Refuge, also in Paris. His influence spread and he was invited to co-operate with the Brazilian architects Oscar Niemeyer et Lucio Costa on the construction of the Ministry of National Education in Rio de Janeiro.

28-29 : A New Age. When? Despite his wish to see a modern society better adapted to human needs, Le Corbusier perceived the rising dangers of militarism and war. He published a book entitled, *Canons, Arms? No thank you! Housing... Yes please,* and created a new pavilion, the Pavilion of the New Era, which reaffirmed the principles of his vision of modernity.

30-31 : The Athens Charter and the CIAM. In 1944, he organized an architects' conference with an association called the CIAM, the International Congress of Modern Architects. These meetings resulted in the Athens Charter, a document that determined the rules and aims of town planning at the time.

32-33 : Housing blocks. Finally, after the war, Le Corbusier was given a commission that allowed him to apply the theory he had been developing since he was twenty years old: the "unité d'habitation" (housing block) in Marseilles, France, a new residential area incorporating housing, social services and even an internal street. He used the same model several times in various French cities.

34-35 : The Modulor. But it is human beings who are always at the heart of his thinking and for Le Corbusier the construction of housing and cities must always be centred on them. He created a mathematical model, the Modulor, which permitted the design of spaces based on the measurements of the human body. The length of the arms, of the legs, and all the elements of the human body thus became the reference point for designing the height of a wall and the scale of buildings.

36-37 : Chandigarh. Finally, in India Le Corbusier was given the opportunity to apply his ideas to a city. The authorities of the Punjab, an Indian state, asked him to build them a new capital, Chandigarh. Criticism rained down on him, but the city was built and remains one of the great examples of an ideal modern city.

38-39 : Religious works. However, Le Corbusier's work was evolving at that time and he was invited to build a chapel at Ronchamp in the Vosges: Notre-Dame du Haut. It is white and rounded, and the most sculptural of his work. A few years later he also built a convent at La Tourette, a more austere building.

40-41 : Late work: the Carpenter Center. Among the great commissions of Le Corbusier's late years is the Carpenter Center for the Visual Arts at Harvard University, Cambridge, Mass., his only building in the United States.

42-43 : The end. Le Corbusier died on 27th August 1965, near his small house at Cap St. Martin on the shores of the Mediterranean.

Contents

Bibliography

About Le Corbusier :
- *Le Corbusier, Œuvre Complète, 1910-1965, (Complete Works, 1910-1965)*, several vols. by Willy Boesiger, Erlenbach-Zurich, Les Éditions d'architecture.
- *Le Corbusier lui-même*, Jean Petit, Geneva, Éditions Rousseau, 1970.
- *Le Corbusier: une Encyclopédie, (Le Corbusier: An Encyclopedia)*, Paris, Éditions du Centre Pompidou, ed. Jacques Lucan, 1987.
- *Le Corbusier (I, II et III)*, video-documentary, directed by Jacques Barzac, production: CIST, A2, Gaumont, INA, La Sept.

By Le Corbusier :
- *Vers une architecture*, Paris, Éditions Crès et Cie, 1923, trans. as *Towards a New Architecture*, London, John Rodker Publisher, 1931.
- *Précisions sur un état présent de l'architecture*, Éditions G. Crès, Paris, 1930, trans. as *Precisions on the Present State of Architecture*, Cambridge, MIT, 1991.
- *L'Art décoratif d'aujourd'hui*, Éditions G. Crès, Paris, 1926, trans. by James I. Dunnett as *The Decorative Art of Today*, Cambridge, MIT, 1987.
- *Lettres à Auguste Perret, (Letters to Auguste Perret)* edition prepared by Marie-Jeanne Dumont, Éditions du Linteau, 2002.

Acknowledgments...

Our warm thanks to Michel Richard and Isabelle Godineau
of the Fondation Le Corbusier for their valuable assistance.
Many thanks also to Fanette Mellier for her work on the font *Futurenner*,
an original design based on Renner's *Futura*, which is used in this book.
We are very grateful to Professor Colin Fournier for checking the English translation.

Credits

6-7. **Image:** Le Corbusier © FLC L4(16)52.
Text: *Le Corbusier lui-même (The Real Le Corbusier)*, Jean Petit.

8-9. **Images:** Orient sketchbook n° 3-1911 © FLC corbu-sketchbook-2; Orient sketch-book n° 3-1911 © FLC corbu-sketchbook-5 ; Orient sketchbook n° 3 - 1911 © FLC corbu-sketchbook 4; drawing 2455, House in Istanbul © FLC corbu-sketchbook-6.
Texts: *Le Voyage d'Orient (Journey to the East)*, Le Corbusier; *Le Corbusier-lui-même*; *Vers une architecture*, Le Corbusier, Paris, Editions Crès et Cie, 1923, trans. as *Towards a New Architecture*, London, John Rodker Publisher, 1931.

10-11. **Images:** Saint-Nicolas d'Aliermont, Cité ouvrière (workers' housing) 1917 © FLC corbu-nob-archi-8(L3(7)1); La Chaux-de-Fonds: Villa Schwob 1916 © FLC L3(16)63; Pessac: Cité Frusés 1924, © FLC CORBU-PES-SAC.
Texts: *Le Corbusier lui-même.*

12-13. **Images:** Cover of Aircraft 1935 © FLC CORBU-AIR; Palace of the League of Nations, Geneva, 1927, Plan FLC 23194 © FLC CORBU-CARNET-7; Cover of the first number of the magazine *L'Esprit Nouveau (The New Spirit)*, 1920 © FLC.
Texts : *The Decorative Art of Today*, Le Corbusier; *Towards a New Architecture.*

14-15. **Images:** The Dom-Ino House, 1914, Plan FLC 19209 © FLC; The Dom-Ino House, 1914, Plan FLC 19221 © FLC.
Texts: *Towards a New Architecture*; *L'Esprit Nouveau (The New Spirit)*, 1920.

16-17. **Images:** Painting FLC 163, *Taureau (Bull) IX-1954* © FLC CORBU-PEINT-1; Sculpture FLC 40, *Panurge*, 1964 © FLC CORBU-SCULP ; Le Corbusier on board the Patris II © FLC I4(7)13.
Texts: *Le Corbusier lui-même.*

18-19. **Images:** Poissy: Villa Savoy, 1928 © FLC CORBU-SAVOYE; Paris: building, 24 rue Nungesser and Coli 1931, Plan FLC 13355 © FLC CORBU-PLAN-4; Paris: building, rue Nungesser and Coli, Le Corbusier's apartment, 1931, Plan FLC 13353 © FLC CORBU-PLAN-3; Taken from the book *La maison des hommes (A House fit for Humans)*, 1942, Archive FLC B3(3)200 © FLC.
Texts: *Towards a New Architecture*; *Precisions on the Present State of Architecture*, Le Corbusier, Third conference ; *Canons, Arms? No thank you! Housing... Yes please*, Le Corbusier.

20-21. **Image:** Paris: Salon d'Automne (Autumn Exhibition), 1929 © FLC.
Texts: *Le Corbusier (I, II et III)*, video-documentary, directed by Jacques Barzac, Production: CIST, A2, Gaumont, INA, La Sept.

22-23. **Image :** A modern city with three million inhabitants, 1922 © FLC L3(20)1.
Texts: *Towards a New Architecture*; *Precisions on the Present State of Architecture*, Le Corbusier, Fourth conference.

24-25. **Images:** *The Radiant City*, 1930, Plan FLC 24909 © FLC CORBU-PLAN-5; Rio de Janeiro: Urbanism, 1929, Plan FLC 32091, © FLC; Lectures by Le Corbusier 1929, Plan FLC 30301 © FLC; Paris: Development of the Porte Maillot 1929, Plan FLC 15047 © FLC.
Texts: *Canons, Arms?; Le Corbusier (I, II et III)*, video-documentary.

26-27. **Images:** Le Corbusier and Joséphine Baker © FLC L5(2)20 ; Moscow: Palace of the Soviets, 1930, Plan FLC 27244© FLC; Moscow: Palace of the Soviets, 1930 © FLC L3(19)41.
Texts: American Foreword to *Precisions on the Present State of Architecture*, Le Corbusier.

28-29. **Images:** Cover of *Canons, Arms?* 1938 © FLC; Paris: Pavilion of the New Era 1937 © FLC; Cartesian Skyscraper 1937 © FLC L3(20)11.
Texts: *On the four methods of transport*, Le Corbusier; *Canons, Arms?*

30-31. **Images:** Le Corbusier on board the Patris II, 1933 © FLC L4(7)12; on board the Patris II, 1933 © FLC L4(7)21.
Texts: *The Athens Charter*, Transport; *The Athens Charter*, Ethics; *The Athens Charter*, Housing.

32-33. **Images:** Marseilles: Unité d'habitation, 1945 © FLC LI(4)20; Marseilles: Unité d'habitation, 1945 © FLC LI(14)6; Marseille: Unité d'habitation, 1945 © FLC.
Texts: *Precisions on the present state of architecture*, Le Corbusier, Fourth conference, a cell on a human scale; *Le Corbusier (I, II et III)*, video-documentary.

34-35. **Image:** The Modulor, 1945 © FLC.
Texts: *Towards a New Architecture*; *The Modulor*, Le Corbusier.

36-37. **Images:** Chandigarh: The Open Hand, 1950-1965 © FLC L3(13)155 ; Chandigarh: The High Court, 1952 © FLC L3(11)94; Chandigarh: The High Court, 1952 © FLC L3(11)50.
Texts: *Le Corbusier lui-même*; *Le Corbusier (I, II et III)*, video-documentary.

38-39. **Images:** Chapel at Ronchamp, 1950 © FLC CORBU RONCHAMP; Eveux: Convent at La Tourette, 1953 © FLC.
Texts: *Le Corbusier lui-même.*

40-41. **Images:** Ahmedabad: Museum, 1956 © FLC L3(8)56; Cambridge, Mass.: Carpenter Visual Arts Center, 1961 © FLC L1(5)23.
Texts: *Le Corbusier lui-même.*

42-43. **Images:** Le Corbusier in his small house at Roquebrune-Cap-Martin © FLC L3(5)5 ; Roquebrune-Cap-Martin: Le Corbusier's grave, 1955 © FLC.
Texts: *Decorative Art of Today.*

All images are © A.D.A.G.P.

First published in Great Britain in 2009 by
Papadakis Publisher

PAPADAKIS

An imprint of New Architecture Group Ltd.
All rights reserved
Head Office: Kimber Studio, Winterbourne, Berkshire, RG20 8AN
www.papadakis.net

ISBN: 978 1901092 981

English edition © 2009, Papadakis Publisher
Publishing Director: Alexandra Papadakis
Translated and edited by Sheila de Vallée
Design Assistant: Hayley Williams

© 2005, Mango for Betty Bone illustrations
Series Director: Jean Poderos; Editorial Assistant: Christian Nobial
Graphic Design: Betty Bone

Printed in France by Pollina - n° L48894